HOW TO WEAR
JEWELRY

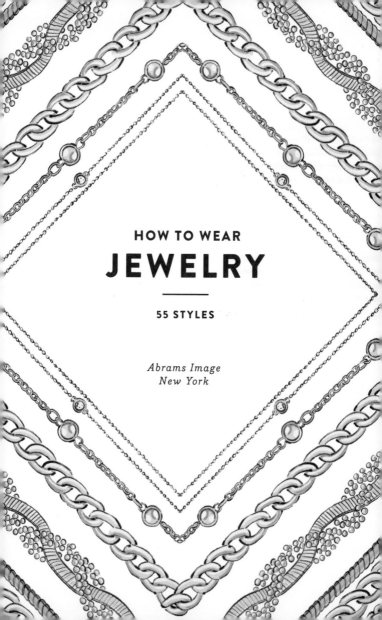

HOW TO WEAR

JEWELRY

55 STYLES

Abrams Image
New York

Table of CONTENTS

INTRODUCTION

Throughout the ages, jewelry has served as symbolic totems and as a creative outlet to embellish appearance. From ancient Egyptian amulets believed to ward off evil to the infamous ropes of pearls favored by Coco Chanel, the function and style of jewelry has evolved, but its glittering presence has remained steadfast.

HOW TO WEAR JEWELRY presents a range of styles for everyone—opulent costume showstoppers; whimsical, barely there pieces; traditional pieces set in classic materials—and offers inventive ways to wear necklaces, bracelets, earrings, brooches, rings, and more. Whether you're a seasoned bauble hoarder or a novice ready to kick-start a collection, consider this a guide to inspire your *bijoux* for years to come.

CHAPTER
ONE

SIGNATURE STYLES

Icons + Inspiration

SIMPLY CLASSIC

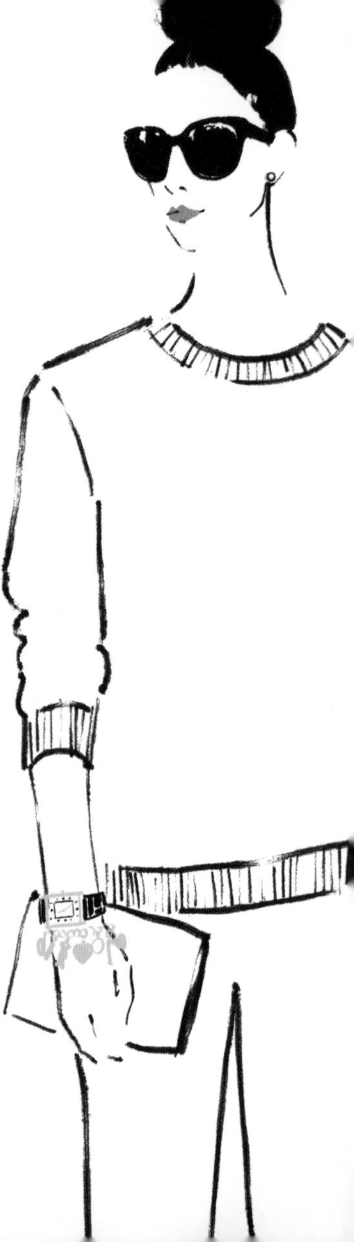

Elegant pearls, tasteful diamond touches, and a few well-chosen pieces for the wrist—classic jewelry never goes out of style. It's no wonder single strands of pearls and sets of diamond earrings have been coveted standby items for generations; they quickly elevate and refine any look.

SIGNATURE PIECES

PEARL NECKLACES // DIAMOND STUDS // PEARL BROOCHES // GOLD BANGLES AND CUFFS // TENNIS BRACELETS // CHARM BRACELETS // SIGNET RINGS

CURATED COSTUME

More is more and nothing is off-limits—including sparkling bracelets, stacks of large geometric rings, clusters of heirloom pins, and maxed-out chunky necklaces. But don't mistake the magpie approach for lowbrow or lazy—every costume piece is carefully selected, and when worn together, the combination transforms into an artful work worthy of appreciation.

SIGNATURE PIECES

COCKTAIL RINGS // LARGE COLLAR NECKLACES // OVERSIZE BROOCHES // MULTI-STRAND NECKLACES WITH SEMIPRECIOUS STONES // STACKABLE BANGLES

ARTFULLY MINDED

Geometric pendants, abstract drop earrings, angular rings—these are the jewelry pieces that could be considered modern art in their own rights. It's these bold pieces that add the final touch to a black-on-black ensemble or bring additional depth to a colorful outfit. When the pieces are carefully selected, the artfully minded jewelry wearer becomes a bona fide curator.

SIGNATURE PIECES

GEOMETRIC PENDANTS AND RINGS // SQUARE BANGLES // ABSTRACT PINS // MARBLE MOTIFS // CUBIC-CUT GEMSTONES

UPDATED HEIRLOOM

Aged rings that bear engraved monograms, gemstone pieces that have been passed down for generations, breathtaking antique finds that have been unearthed at flea markets—these priceless heritage pieces are full of character. Whether your heirloom jewelry is worn on its own or incorporated in with modern pieces, nothing makes an outfit more timeless than antiques.

SIGNATURE PIECES

ANTIQUE RINGS AND NECKLACES // MOURNING JEWELRY // GEMSTONES (onyx, moonstone, and turquoise) // GOLD LOCKETS // VINTAGE BROOCHES

DIY CHIC

Necklaces strung with homemade beads, friendship bracelets woven with care, and custom rings soldered in small studios—the best kinds of jewelry are the ones that are handcrafted with love by the jewelers who designed them. With the resurgence of DIY jewelry and one-of-a-kind designs available in stores and online, these artisanal accessories might just become the new classics.

SIGNATURE PIECES

WOVEN NECKLACES AND BRACELETS // CAST-METAL EARRINGS // WOODEN BANGLES AND BROOCHES // GLASS- AND CLAY-BEAD NECKLACES // FRIENDSHIP BRACELETS

MODERN BOHEMIAN

The modern bohemian invokes whimsy through an eclectic mix of jewelry that is as free-spirited as it is chic. Playfully combining a range of global influences—from a touch of brightly colored turquoise or a dappling of oxidized silver to yards of multicolor beaded necklaces—these pieces create a perfect picture of a stylish bohemian.

SIGNATURE PIECES

WESTERN AND TRIBAL MOTIFS // TURQUOISE AND BEADED NECKLACES // LEATHER AND SILVER CUFFS // CRYSTAL PENDANTS // HEADBANDS

CHAPTER
TWO

NECKLACES

Layer + Twist

Necklaces are true finishing pieces. A colorful statement necklace adds character and interest to simple outfits; considered gold chains and ropes of pearls imbue elegance; multi-layered strands of beads, box chains, and pendants hint to personality and taste.

Here are the most common necklace styles to know:

CHAIN – a long series of metal links that serves as a foundation for necklaces and can be worn solo or with a pendant

PEARL – a string of incandescent beads, derived from pearl oysters and mollusks, that comes in a variety of lengths

CHOKER – a simple necklace—usually made from leather, fabric, or thin metal—that fits snugly around the middle of the neck

PENDANT – an ornamental charm that hangs from a necklace

BIB – a decorative bib-shaped necklace that fits at the collar, usually held together by a series of looped chains

COLLAR – a necklace that fits at the collar of the neck and imitates the neckline of a button-down shirt

STATEMENT – an extravagantly stunning necklace full of colorful pieces or stones that draws attention

MULTI-STRAND – a necklace with more than one strand of pearls or chains attached to the clasp

In the pages ahead, you'll rethink how to style pearls, learn a foolproof way to layer dainty necklaces, see what necklines work best with your pieces, and more.

Great LENGTHS

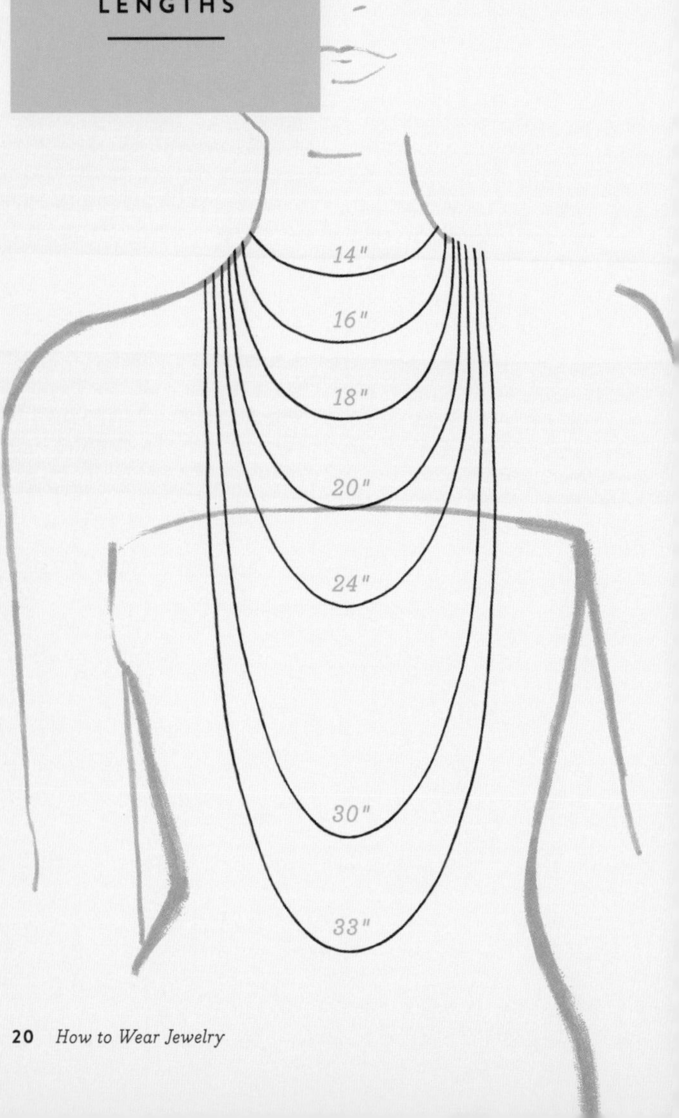

Whether you're choosing a necklace for a night out or building a multi-layered look, these measurements are a simple guide to making it all work.

14" CHOKER

Choker necklaces fit snugly around the middle of your neck.

16" COLLAR

Collar necklaces sit comfortably at the base of your neck, where, as you've guessed, most collars on button-downs finish. Bib necklaces are most associated with the collar length.

18" PRINCESS

The princess necklace gets a bit more breathing room and drops down to the upper-chest area. You'll find plenty of statement necklaces and pendants dangling at this chain length.

20–24" MATINEE

The matinee necklace generally hits mid-chest, and, as the name suggests, leans toward a casual afternoon look. Beaded necklaces and longer pendants tend to fall in this area.

30" OPERA

The opera necklace scoops below the breast and pairs nicely with more formal frocks. Chains and long strands of pearls end at these plunging lengths.

33" ROPE OR LARIAT

The super-long rope necklace is the most dramatic—it hangs near the waist. Vintage necklaces that you can slip on and loop twice around your neck are generally found at this stunning length.

How to
LAYER

DELICATE CHAINS

1

Start with the most delicate piece. Wear the lightest, most-delicate necklace closest to the neck, following with heavier necklaces as you layer.

2

Space out the necklaces. Make sure each piece has breathing room. While the spacing of each necklace doesn't have to follow exact measurements, be mindful that they don't lie on top of one another. Note how the second bar necklace is about a half-inch (12 mm) from the first necklace, but the third necklace hangs an inch (2.5 cm) from the second.

3

Mix metals and textures. Box chains, gold bars, beaded necklaces, and small stones—layer different metals and styles as you go. Note how the beaded necklace second from the bottom adds texture to a look that is mostly made up of chains.

4

Anchor the entire look with your largest pendant. The heaviest pendant and longest chain necklace should always sit at the bottom layer to help anchor the entire look. If you try to layer another necklace below a pendant, the spacing between the necklaces will look unbalanced.

Delicate chains are pretty enough to wear on their own but so much more fun to layer with other dainty necklaces. Once you know the rules of how to pile them on, you can layer your chains in a million ways.

MATERIALLY MAXED OUT

1

Select one centerpiece. Start with your most prominent statement piece as the base. The centerpiece has a bit more weight than the others—it's the one showcased in the middle. Here, the base piece is the stunner that hangs second from the top. See how that one piece does a lot of the heavy lifting? Without it, the look wouldn't be as robust.

2

Layer around the centerpiece. Next, select two additional bold necklaces—one that falls just above the base necklace and one that falls just below it—and layer them on. There will be inevitable overlapping, so just be sure that the necklaces aren't directly on top of one another. (You wouldn't want a collision of those precious stones and that vintage beading!)

3

Add a few easy chains. To finish the look, throw on one or two simple chains of varying lengths to add depth to this massive neck party. Look into wheat chains or box chains—they tend to work best because of their hefty shapes and textures.

How to Style by
SEASON

FALL ▶

An edgy statement necklace is the perfect piece to wear with a soft, silken collared shirt to create nice textural contrast for fall. Wear your statement piece closer to the neck to accentuate the biblike quality of the necklace.

◀ WINTER

Choose pieces that are big enough to compete with a winter coat, and wear them around chunky-knit turtlenecks to complement the weight of your outfits.

Despite its bravado, the statement necklace is easily adaptable year-round. Take a look at how these bold numbers can work through the changing seasons.

SPRING

It's all about florals in the springtime, so pair a jeweled statement bib with a bright shift dress to add an extra punch of color and shine. To liven up a casual look, wear the necklace with a simple white T-shirt.

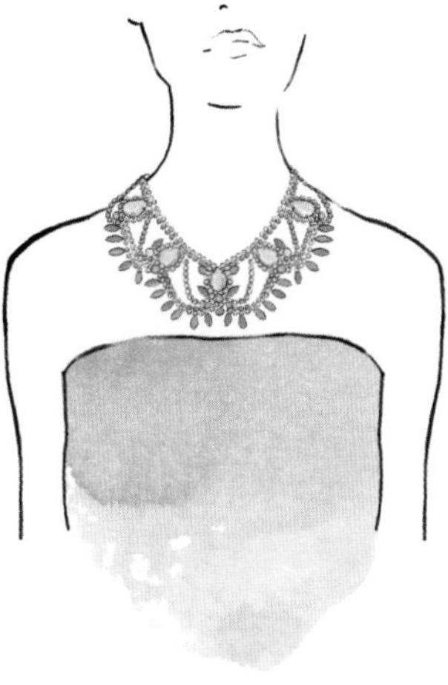

SUMMER

To celebrate the shining summer sun, opt for a statement necklace with electric brights. Limit yourself to wearing just one showpiece (to stay cool), and pair the necklace with a seasonally appropriate strapless top.

NECKLINE
Cheat Sheet

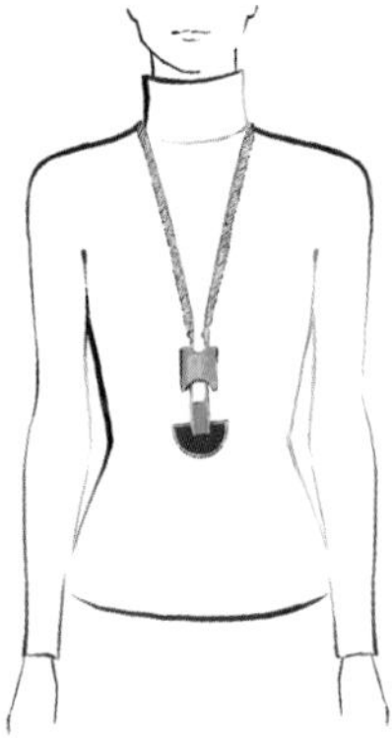

TURTLENECK ▶

Pair a longer necklace with a turtleneck to help elongate your torso.

◀ CREWNECK

A bib necklace works best when it's worn exactly like a bib—over a simple, clean-cut crewneck to play up the effect of a secondary collar.

STRAPLESS ▶

A necklace that peacocks all the way around needs to be seen from every angle, ideal for a strapless look.

If you've ever questioned which necklines work best with your necklaces (or ever wondered which would best show off a beloved piece), let this visual cheat sheet be your foolproof guide.

SQUARE NECK ▶

If you've got a square or boxy pendant to flaunt, showcase it with a corresponding square neckline to match the geometric shape of the charm.

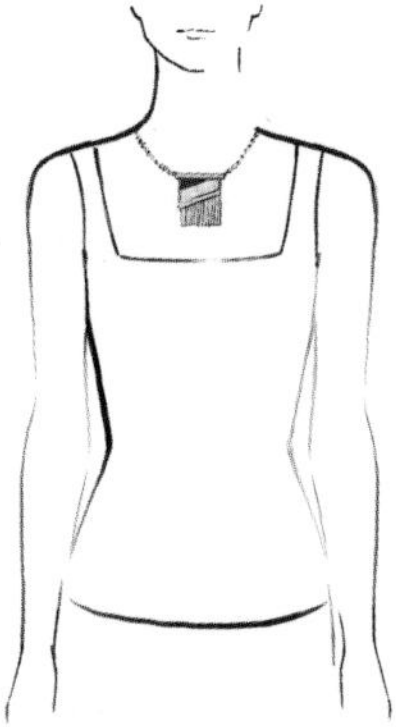

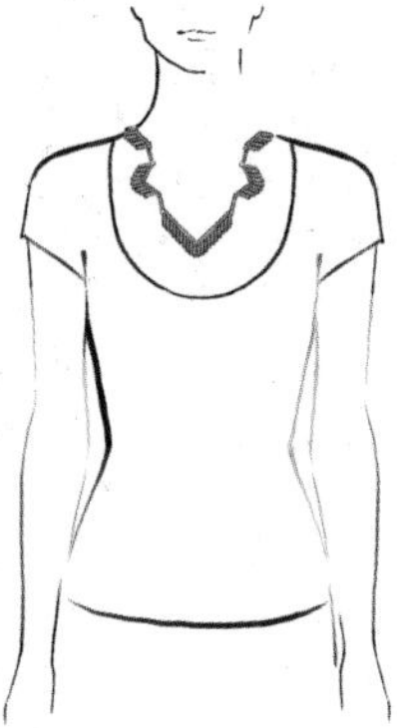

◀ SCOOP NECK

Pair a decorative, U-shaped necklace with a similarly rounded scoop neck—the neckline won't impede the ornate pendants.

BOATNECK

For an unexpected way to showcase long, beaded necklaces, wear them over a wide boatneck revealing a hint of shoulder.

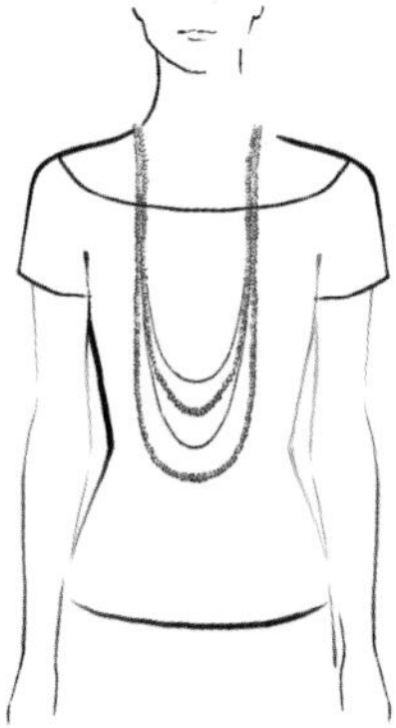

How to Wear
PEARLS

KNOTTED

Knotting your jewelry is normally not encouraged, but with a long strand of pearls, it's an easy way to transform a simple necklace.

HOW TO STYLE

If you're keen on wearing a menswear-inspired pantsuit, pearls bring a touch of femininity. Keep them knotted to maintain a streamlined look.

Pearls, as lovely and timeless as they are, can sometimes get a bad rap for being too formal. So we're twisting up these long ivory gems for a new take on the classic.

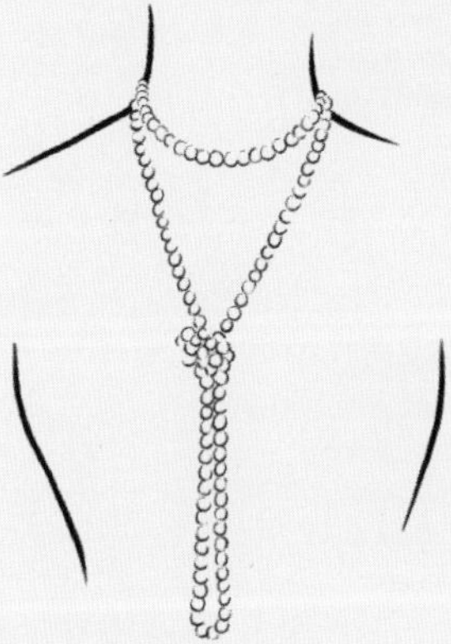

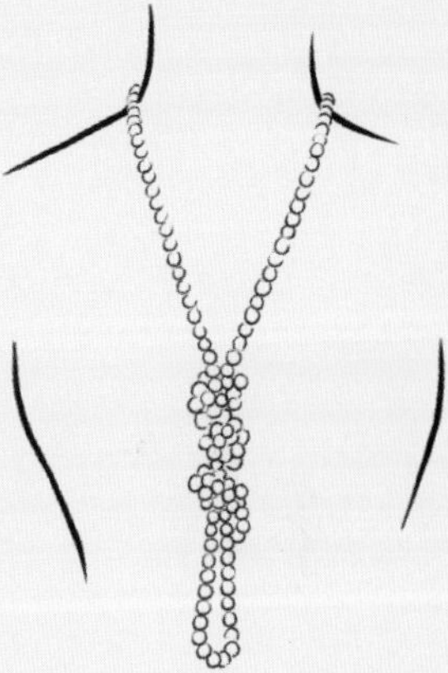

// VARIATIONS //

1 *Loop a long strand of pearls twice around your neck. Adjust the two strands so the bottom loop sits matinee length (approximately 20 inches / 50 cm). Tie a knot in the bottom loop to create a "loosened-tie" look.*

2 *If a single knot isn't doing it for you, give your strand multiple knots to create larger pearl clusters. You can either keep knotting over the same one knot for a snowball effect or knot in succession for a more uniform approach.*

PINNED

Nothing elevates a set of pearls more than adding an ornate pin or brooch. Opt for a decently sized pin in a complementing metal or decorated with non-clashing semiprecious stones.

HOW TO STYLE

Embellish a ladylike look by adding a pinned pearl necklace. The pearl-and-gemstone combination is an easy way to bring more detail to a simple dress.

// VARIATIONS //

1 *Loop your pearls so they sit in three lengths and pin a flowery brooch with gemstones or pearls directly onto your sweater to keep the desired length in place.*

2 *Loop your pearls twice to have the double strands sit at opera length and use a single floral brooch to pin them together. Attach the pin near the chest area, where you'd normally pin a brooch.*

TWISTED

Give your strands a modern update with a super-messy twist that will make you look mighty put-together.

HOW TO STYLE

Liven up a blazer/sweater combo with a set of twisted pearls. For additional texture, layer these pearls with a gemstone necklace under a shirt collar—the satin finish of pearls contrasts nicely with the sparkle of gems.

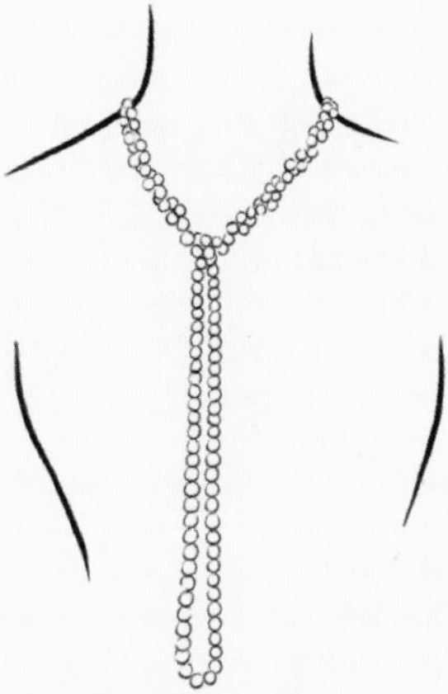

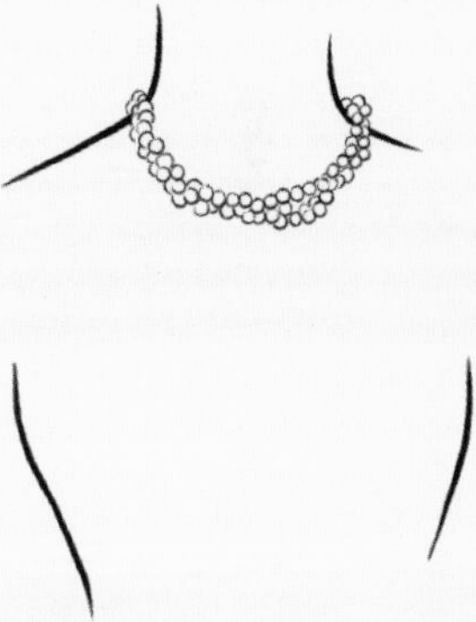

// VARIATIONS //

1 *You'll recognize the basic pull-through—a common scarf-tying move that involves pulling one end of the necklace through the loop of the other end. To add much-needed interest and movement, simply twist a chokerlike set of pearls a few times.*

2 *Fold a long strand of pearls in half and twist the ends around in opposite directions until it shortens to fit comfortably around the base of your neck. Wrap the twisted set of pearls and use a small brooch or pin as a clasp to attach the two ends together at the back of the neck.*

How to Wear a REVERSE NECKLACE

The backward necklace, the reverse necklace, the backdrop—no matter what you call it, this dramatic turn-it-around style was a favorite of Coco Chanel, who wore her ropes of pearls backward. Remember, the whole point is to show off these back skimmers, so pull your hair forward or into a fine updo.

LARGE PENDANT ▶

Keep it ultrasimple with two or three medium-size pieces. Select one short necklace and one long necklace, with about two inches separating them, and play around with varying pendant shapes and chain textures.

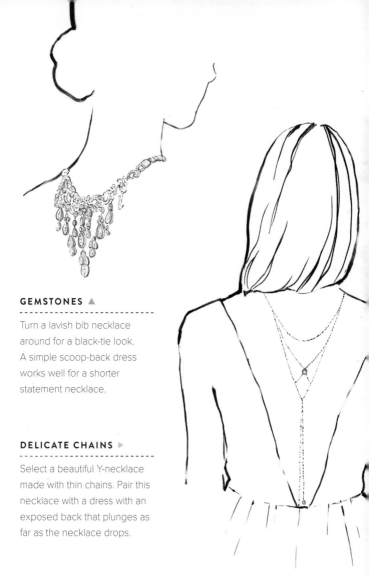

GEMSTONES ▲

Turn a lavish bib necklace around for a black-tie look. A simple scoop-back dress works well for a shorter statement necklace.

DELICATE CHAINS ▶

Select a beautiful Y-necklace made with thin chains. Pair this necklace with a dress with an exposed back that plunges as far as the necklace drops.

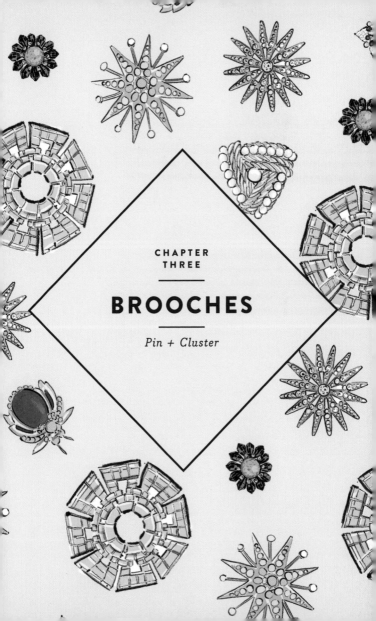

CHAPTER THREE

BROOCHES

Pin + Cluster

Brooches and pins are the hardest-working pieces of jewelry. These bijoux *are not only beautiful embellishments, but also markers of clubs and societies, historical bearers of lineage, and functional pieces that hold garments together with style.*

Here are the most common brooches and pins to know:

STICK PIN—a small, delicate, lollipoplike brooch attached with a longer stick pin

CAMEO—an intricate carving, usually of a woman's profile, traditionally carved from a semiprecious gemstone such as onyx or agate

ANNULAR—a piece circular in shape that has the pin running across the diameter of the brooch

HAIR—a brooch that incorporates the hair of a passed love one into the design, also know as mourning jewelry

VINTAGE—a pin that originates from a previous era

LAPEL PIN—a small enamel pin usually worn on the lapel of a jacket or other outerwear to represent membership to an organization

In this chapter, we take a gander at the inventive ways your brooch collection can enhance a garment, breathe new life into accessories, and end up in unexpected places.

How to
CLUSTER BROOCHES

THEMED COLLECTIONS

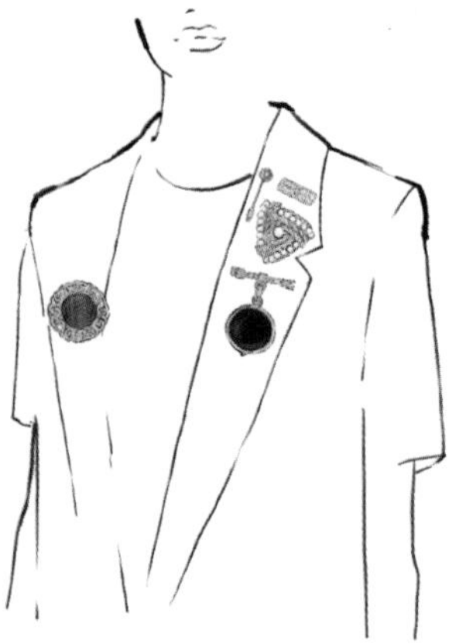

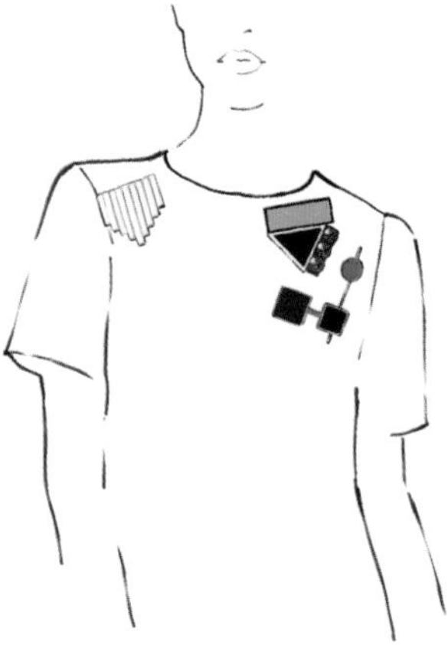

VINTAGE GOLD

If you're looking to class up your office attire in a jiffy, select any number of vintage gold brooches—look for tigereye stones, pearls, gems, and sunburst stick pins—and attach them to the lapel of a blazer for an easy upgrade.

GEOMETRIC

If your neutral outfit is in need of a little boost, opt for pins that feature strong geometric shapes, asymmetry, or expert colorblocking.

Whether you stick to vintage semiprecious stones or prefer colorful floral pins, there's a brooch out there for everyone.

FLORAL

Make it a garden party and pin several flowery brooches onto a light jacket. To keep floral pins from looking precious, attach them to a tougher fabric such as denim to keep things casual.

INSECTS

Nobody wants a bug crawling around on their shoulders, but bejeweled critters are another story. For a real conversation starter, pin a few gorgeous bug brooches on a clean slate such as a white top.

If you've got 'em, flaunt 'em. For a powerful punch, pin on an overload of brooches, concentrated on the shoulders and chest.

1

Wear a sturdy blazer jacket. Choose a jacket with thick fabric—like heavy tweed, corduroy, or denim—that will support the weight of the brooches.

2

Mix and match metals. To keep the brooches looking cohesive, stick to similar-looking metals such as all silver, brass, or gold, or a mix of complementing metals that are matte or shiny.

3

Work around the anchor pieces. When creating the maxed-out brooch look, start with your two largest statement brooches and pin each of them to a different side of the blazer. These will serve as the anchors.

4

Surround the anchored pieces with smaller pins. Space out the medium-size brooches on both sides of the blazer and fill in any gaps with smaller pins as finishing pieces.

5

Create symmetry. To find a balanced look, aim to form as much symmetry as possible on both sides of the blazer. This means dividing equal amounts of medium- and small-size pieces on both sides.

6

Max it out. Select a range of materials: diamond brooches, pearl pins, modern designs, vintage motifs, and a variety of gemstone colors that complement the overall theme.

How to Wear

COLLAR PINS+ CHAINS

POINTED COLLAR PINS ▶

For subtle embellishment, attach collar pins—one on each collar tip—to bedazzle a dress shirt. Keep necklaces to a minimum to make these pins really stand out.

◀ MAXED-OUT CHAIN BROOCHES

An elegant way to dress up an oxford shirt is to attach a maxed-out chain brooch—multiple chains, ornamental pins—for ultimate collar flair.

Jazzing up the collar of your button-down has never been so easy. Button your shirt all the way up and attach these collar pins for a simple upgrade.

JEWELED COLLAR PINS ▸

If you don't have pointed collar pins, select two similar lapel pins or smaller brooches that can still attach to the collar. Diamond or silver brooches look stunning on silk shirts.

◂ SIMPLE CHAIN BROOCHES

Make a crisp white oxford more interesting with a simple chain brooch. The embellishment looks particularly on point if you're wearing the top tucked into black trousers.

How to Style by SEASON

SPRING ▶

Get out your enamel floral brooches and line them up around the neckline of your favorite dress to create an eclectic and colorful arrangement.

◀ FALL

There's nothing like a bejeweled vintage brooch to add that touch of personalization to an autumn sweater. Position your brooch directly under your collar for a snug fit.

Here's how to make brooches work with your outfits every season. Whether you're bundled up or removing layers, brooches can add a much-needed accent to any ensemble.

WINTER ▸

Go big and bold with two matching oversize brooches on a collared coat. Heavy-duty brooches work best for this look since delicate brooches risk getting broken.

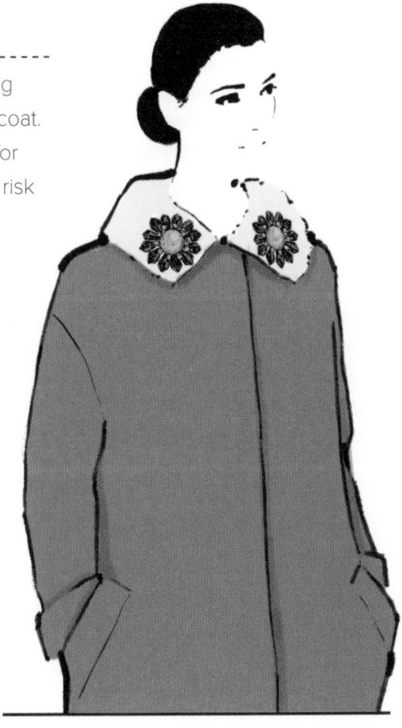

◂ SUMMER

Keep it simple for summer—if you're wearing a collared shirt, adorn the collar tips with a chain brooch.

How to Wear
BROOCHES + NECKLACES

Since single brooches tend to look lonesome on a top or a sweater, pair one with a necklace to take your outfit to the next level.

BIG GEMS

Pair a vintage gem brooch with a statement necklace to boost the sparkle factor. Rather than wearing the brooch on your chest, attach it between the points of your button-down collar like a bow. The symmetry of the brooch with a jeweled bib necklace looks particularly polished.

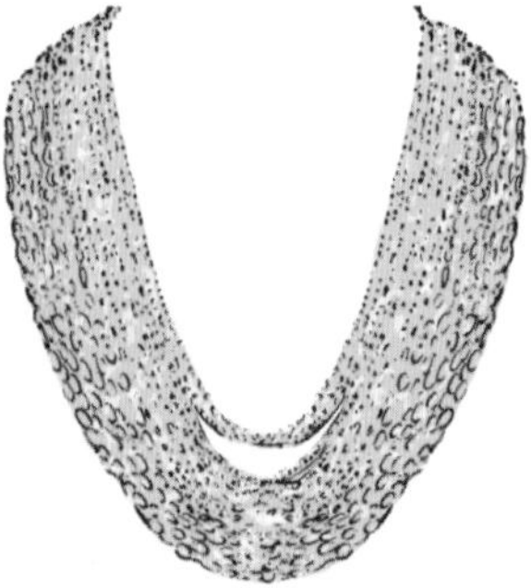

OLD-SCHOOL CHARM

If you're looking to find a necklace companion for your classic pin of gold, pearls, and black leather, match it with chunky strands of gold chain links. This combo works well because the chains in the necklaces match the link shape and color of the pin.

DELICATE LAYERS

A delicate pin like the one shown above—an arrow with a thin decorative chain hanging from it—is pretty on its own, but its daintiness can get lost easily on a sweater. Pair a smaller pin with a tiered necklace, as these pieces will simultaneously complement and enhance each other.

Put a Pin ON IT

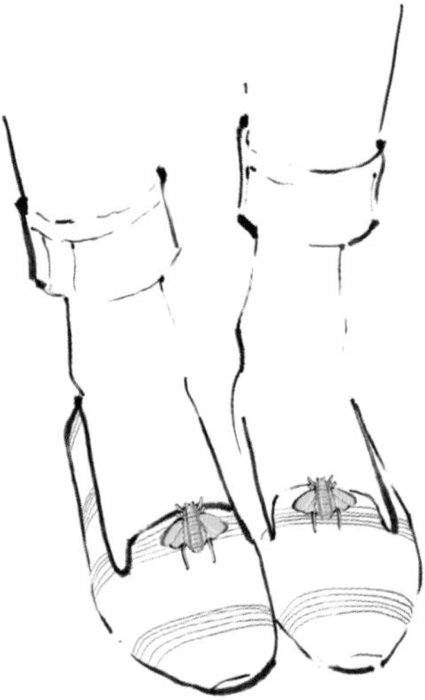

ON YOUR LOAFERS ▸

Grab a set of small insect pins and attach them to your shoes for fancy feet. Fabric loafers make excellent candidates since they tend to hold pins far better than other shoe materials, such as leather. Plus, you can remove the pins at the end of the day and your shoes won't be ruined.

◂ ON YOUR SCARF

Add some fun to your chunky knit scarf by attaching a large vintage brooch to it (the pin can also work to keep your scarf in place). Keep the brooch pinned to the side to achieve a subtle touch of embellishment.

It's as easy as it sounds! Discover ways to easily embellish your other accessories just by pinning them creatively.

ON YOUR HAT ▶

Accentuate your hat with a quirky pin—it adds character to what would otherwise be just another basic accessory. This works all year round, too: You can pin a floral brooch to a straw hat or attach a vintage gemstone brooch to a winter beanie.

▲ IN YOUR HAIR

You can attach barrettes, bobby pins, or a hair comb to a brooch to secure it in your hair. Another tactic involves pinning a brooch to a long piece of ribbon that can then be used as a headband.

CHAPTER FOUR

BRACELETS

Pile + Clasp

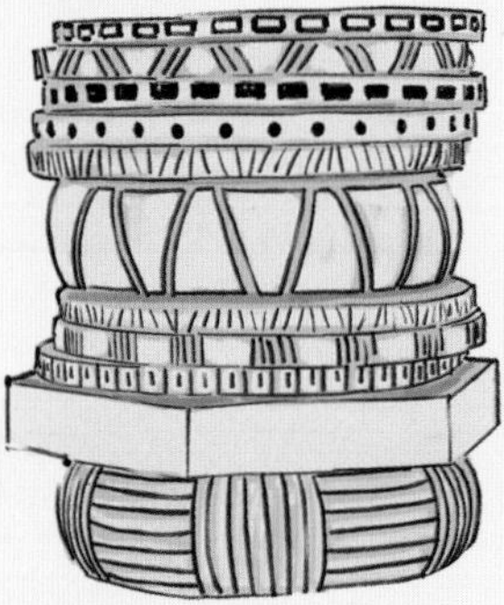

Bracelets are versatile pieces of jewelry that can play more than a supporting role dependent on style. Large artful cuffs, Fifth Avenue enamel, plastic bangles, and delicate gold links can be worn solo, stacked unexpectedly, or doubled on each wrist for maximum effect—there are limitless ways to reimagine the bracelet.

Here are the most common bracelet styles to know:

CUFF—a wide split metal bracelet that fits right over the wrist

BANGLE—a usually non-flexible hoop bracelet to be slipped over the entire hand

CHAIN—a linked-metal bracelet of a variety of styles, including box, figaro, snake, wheat, and rope shapes

CHARM—a chain bracelet with very large links from which charms and trinkets hang

DIAMOND—a fine metal bracelet with individually set diamonds that go all the way around (also known as a tennis bracelet)

FRIENDSHIP—a DIY bracelet made from a series of colorfully knotted threads or strands of yarn

Read on for the lowdown on how to master the ultimate bracelet stack, how to style bracelets for the changing seasons, and the best way to build around a simple leather band. Whether you're looking for a way to adorn your naked wrist or you're in the mood to switch up your everyday arm look, you're sure to find a bracelet style that stacks up to your taste.

How to
STACK

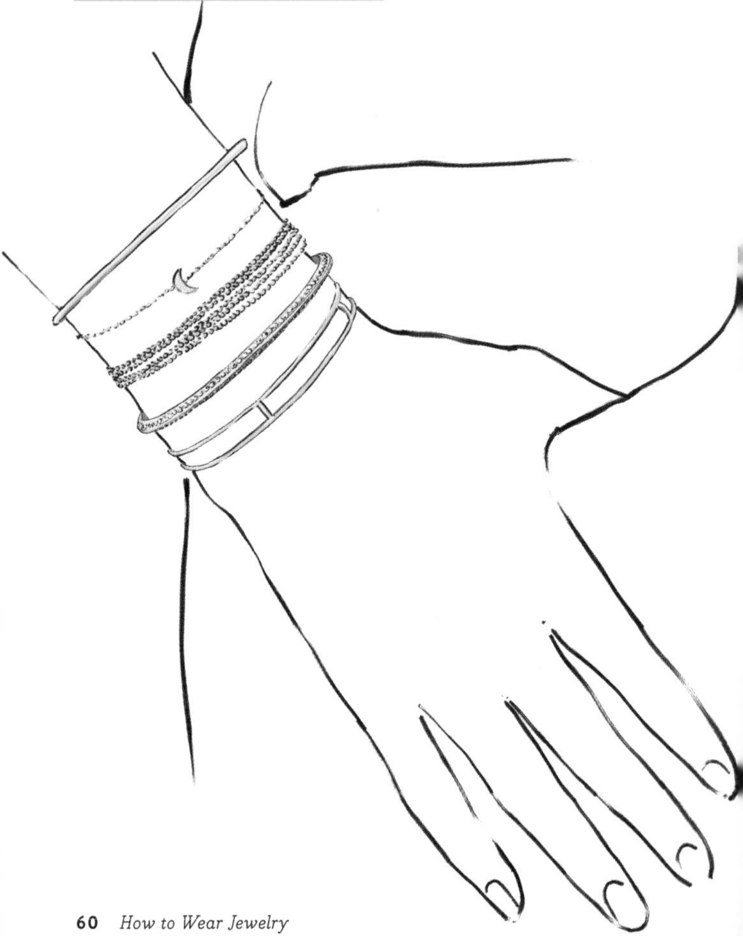

Stacking bangles, chains, straps, charms, and cuffs is a simple way to mix up your collection. Whether you prefer a delicate look or want to pile on the statement pieces, use the style breakdown below to help update your bracelet game.

THE DELICATE STACK

1

Start with delicates. Select similar bracelets—thin chains, bangles, and cuffs—that fit snugly around your wrist. Bracelets that are too thick overcrowd the wrist and add weight.

2

Mix bracelet styles and textures. Note how each of these bracelets is slightly different. Selecting a variety of styles—chains, bangles, diamonds—helps diversify the look.

3

Space them out according to fit. It's best to dress up your wrist based on how the bracelets fit. Bangles are nonadjustable and tend to be on the bigger side, so keep them higher on the arm, whereas daintier, adjustable bracelets can rest closer to the hand.

4

Go easy on diamonds. The key to any delicate stack is subtlety and proportion—limit yourself to one super-sparkly bangle if the other stackables are low-key.

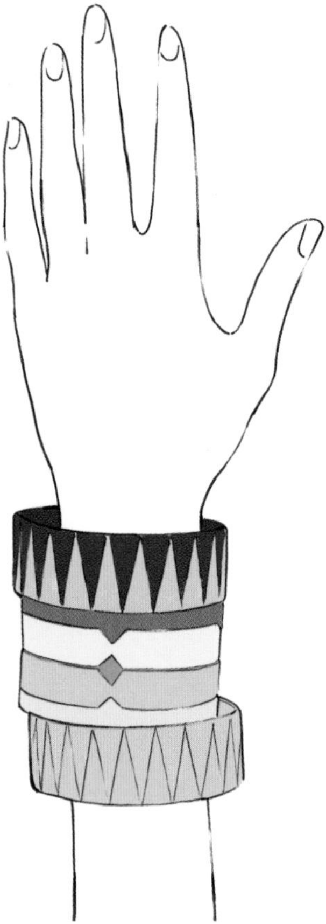

◀ THE ENAMEL STACK

Select your bangles. Select up to three styles similar in width, design, and palette to keep the look cohesive.

Double the fun. Stack up the other arm with similar-looking enamel pieces to create a symmetrical look.

Wear an outfit that complements the stack. Enamel bracelets can be worn casually or more formally, so whether you're wearing a T-shirt or LBD, opt for shorter sleeves to let the bracelets shine.

THE FRIENDSHIP STACK ▶

Choose friendship bracelets turned luxe. Look for pieces that embody the DIY spirit with sophisticated materials such as colorful silk cords, gold beads, and tassels.

Stack them silly. When it comes to mixing multiple friendship bracelets, nothing beats a carefree spirit. Pile on the pieces and let them overlap.

Wear an outfit that complements the stack. Wear these colorful bracelets with a vintage T-shirt and a jean jacket with the sleeves rolled.

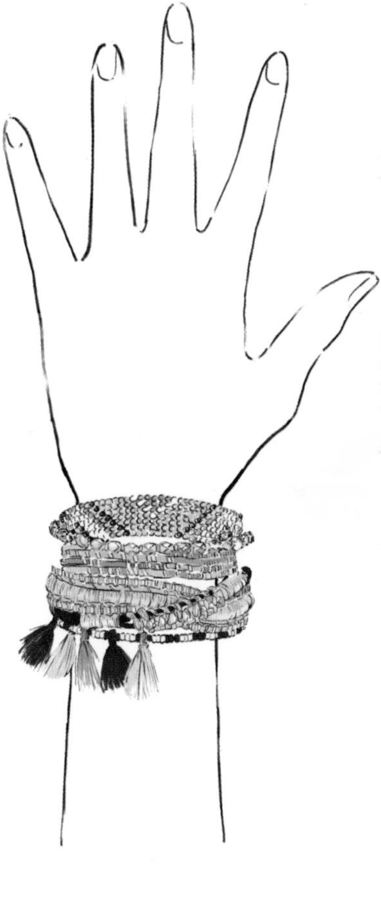

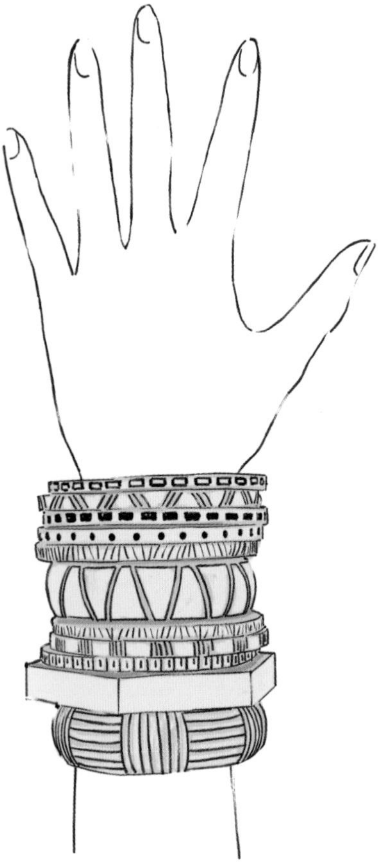

THE PATTERNED-BANGLE STACK

Wild out on patterns. When it comes to printed plastic bangles, select the boldest styles to mix and match while staying in the same color scheme.

Alternate thick and thin. Stack so that thick bangles are interspersed with thinner ones. Notice how the two widest bangles are spaced well apart to retain proportion.

Wear an outfit that complements the stack. Choose a low-key, solid-color dress to showcase the stack or go bold on a similarly patterned-out ensemble.

THE SOUTHWESTERN STACK ▸

Select your silvers. The vibe of the Southwestern stack is simple: turquoise, silver, and Native American–inspired motifs. The silver here isn't highly polished, so choose toned-down finishes such as nickel and oxidized silver.

Stack them strategically. Wear the bracelets as they fit best on the wrist, alternating wide and thin bracelets.

Wear an outfit that complements the stack. Since the Southwestern stack is pretty fine-tuned to the bohemian look, this stack tends to look best with flowy, floral dresses or fringed leather vests.

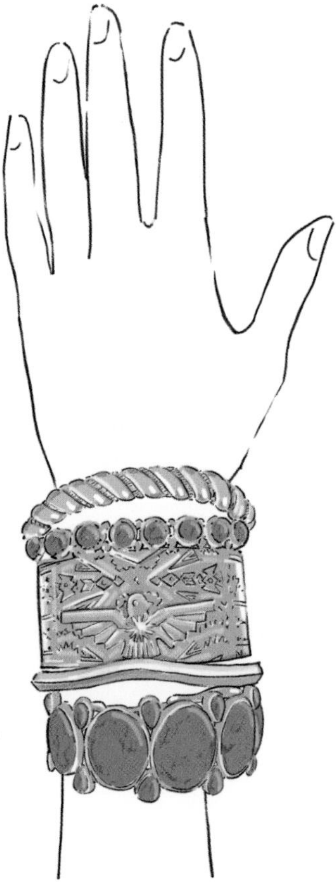

How to Work in a
WATCH

Beginning with a key timepiece, here are the staples you need in your arsenal to create limitless combinations.

1

Start with a watch. Depending on your personal style, select a versatile watch made with materials that will easily lend themselves to your everyday wear. Common watch options include leather or plastic straps, metal or jeweled links, a large or small face, and analog or electronic functionalities.

2

Add an interesting cuff. The cuff may be simple in shape but they can come in many intricate designs. Even if it's your only bracelet, you can always count on a cuff to make your arm look a bit more finished and to complement your watch.

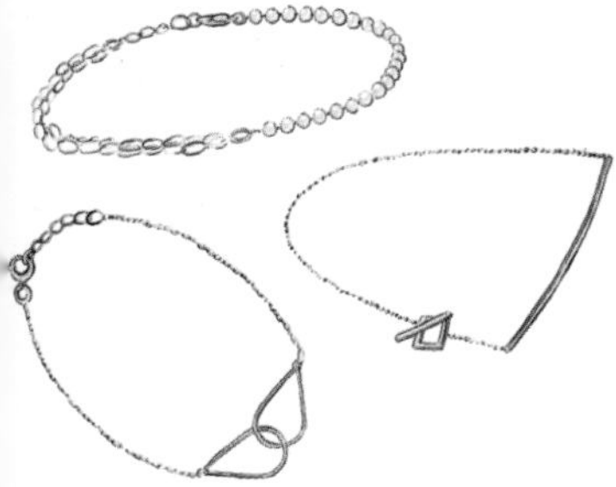

3

Choose a delicate chain or two. Small gold chains rest easily on top of a watch. They're subtle enough for everyday wear and beautifully simple.

4

Throw in a bangle. The one-size fit means there are no pesky clasps to deal with, so it's a must-have piece for watch-stacking purposes.

How to Style by
SEASON

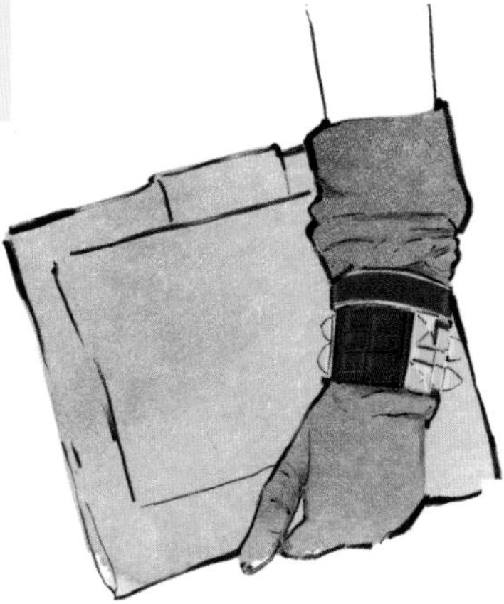

WINTER ▸

To accessorize with winter wear, select a wide, luxe bangle cuff or two to stack over a sleek leather glove for the cold weather.

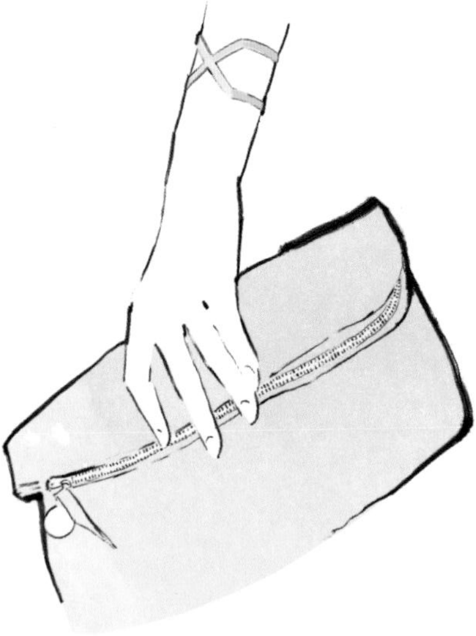

◂ SPRING

Choose a single sculptural metal cuff with cutout details to match the breeziness of a spring outfit.

Even as temperatures rise and fall, there are always opportunities to wear your bracelets.

SUMMER ▶

Summer is all about keeping things light and colorful, so layer delicate beaded bracelets with bright friendship bracelets (or other pieces that won't get too sweaty on your wrist).

◀ FALL

Layer on pieces with oversize gold links, rich leather straps, and lush accented textures like tortoiseshell and wood to reflect autumn's earthy tones.

Two Ways to Wear
GOLD CUFFS

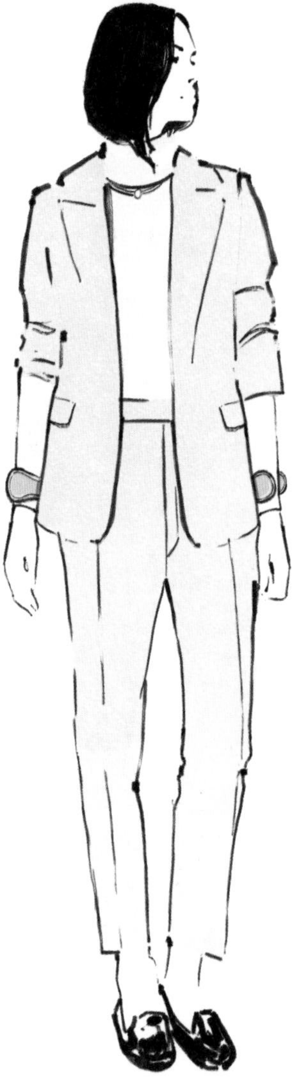

Versatility is key when it comes to investing in a piece of jewelry. Here are two different ways to wear the standard gold cuff bracelet—one for the office-going weekday and the other for the off-duty weekend.

WEEKDAY

For a touch of office bling, wear your gold cuffs over the sleeves of your oxford button-down. Go ahead and roll up the sleeves of your power blazer, too.

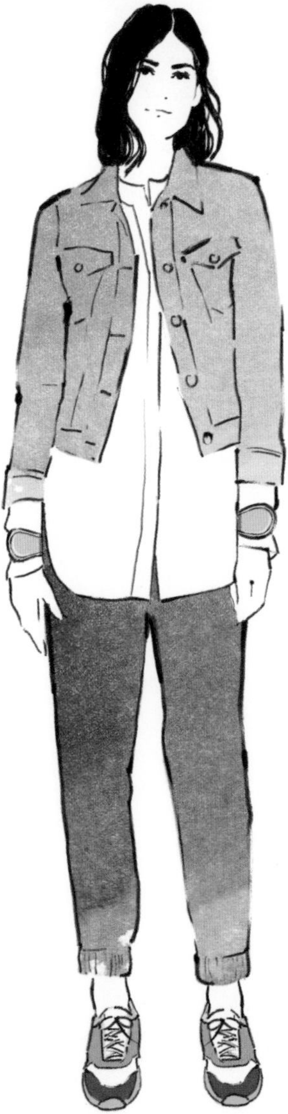

WEEKEND

For a casual afternoon look, slip your gold cuffs over the sleeves of an oversize boyfriend shirt and top off the easy look with a jean jacket.

Three Ways to Wear
LEATHER BANDS

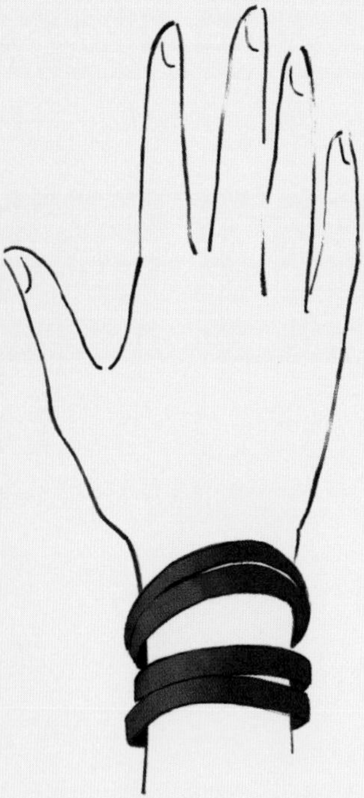

Most people associate leather bands with the straps of their watches. Fair enough; it's the everyday utility of the material that makes leather essential. It's softer than plastic and lighter than metal, and it has a crafty vibe to it. Check out how you can incorporate leather into your everyday stack.

◀ THE SIMPLE STACK

Choose a few thin leather bands to stack on top of one another.

ADD CHAINS ▸

Mix gold and leather to create a deluxe saddle look. Since leather appears a bit more sturdy and heavy-duty, match your metals accordingly and go for oversize gold chain links.

◂ ADD PEARLS

An eclectic way to dress up a leather bracelet or tone down a strand of pearls is to take one of each and wrap them into one harmonious blend.

CHAPTER FIVE

RINGS

Stack + Curate

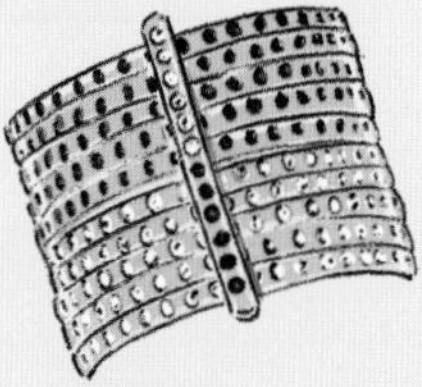

Ornamental and symbolic, these small pieces can hold significant meaning. From engagement showstoppers to traditional signets, rings are often the most personal pieces of any jewelry collection.

Here are the most common ring styles to know:

ENGAGEMENT—a ring, usually set with a diamond or gemstone, that represents engagement for marriage

WEDDING BAND—a ring that is worn after a wedding ceremony to denote marital status

SOLITAIRE—a ring that bears a single gemstone on a plain band

FIDELITY (OR PROMISE)—a ring that signifies relationship status and usually depicts interlocking hands or a knot

ETERNITY RING—a ring that has individually set stones around the band

COCKTAIL (OR COSTUME)—an opulent ring, with one oversize gemstone or semiprecious stone, often made with affordable materials

ANTIQUE—a vintage ring that dates back to an earlier era

FIRST-KNUCKLE RING—a small ring that fits in between the first and second knuckles

SIGNET—a personalized ring bearing an emblem, crest, or initials

CLASS—a ring to signify a membership to a society, group, or institution

Learn how to proportion your delicate rings, see how to do the costume stack in a non-clunky way, discover how to actually wear first-knuckle rings, and more. Get your fingers ready for some glitz and glamour—these looks are ringing with style.

The SIZE GUIDE

Knowing your ring size will come in handy if you're seeking a custom piece, looking to resize an existing ring, or ordering a ring online and cannot try it on in person.

To find your ring size, wrap a piece of string or a thin strip of paper around your finger and mark it. Every finger is shaped differently, so measure the finger on the hand where you intend to wear a particular ring.

Measure your finger's circumference in millimeters and match it to the corresponding ring size shown opposite. If your measurement falls in between numbers, it's recommended you size up. (This sizing method works for first-knuckle rings as well.)

For best results, measure your finger toward the end of the day, when your hands are naturally larger from the day's activities.

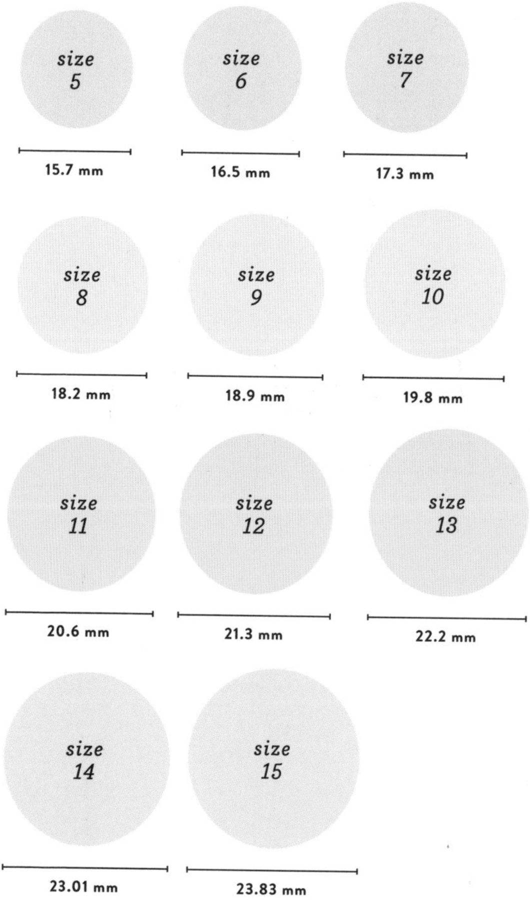
size 5
15.7 mm
size 6
16.5 mm
size 7
17.3 mm
size 8
18.2 mm
size 9
18.9 mm
size 10
19.8 mm
size 11
20.6 mm
size 12
21.3 mm
size 13
22.2 mm
size 14
23.01 mm
size 15
23.83 mm

How to STACK

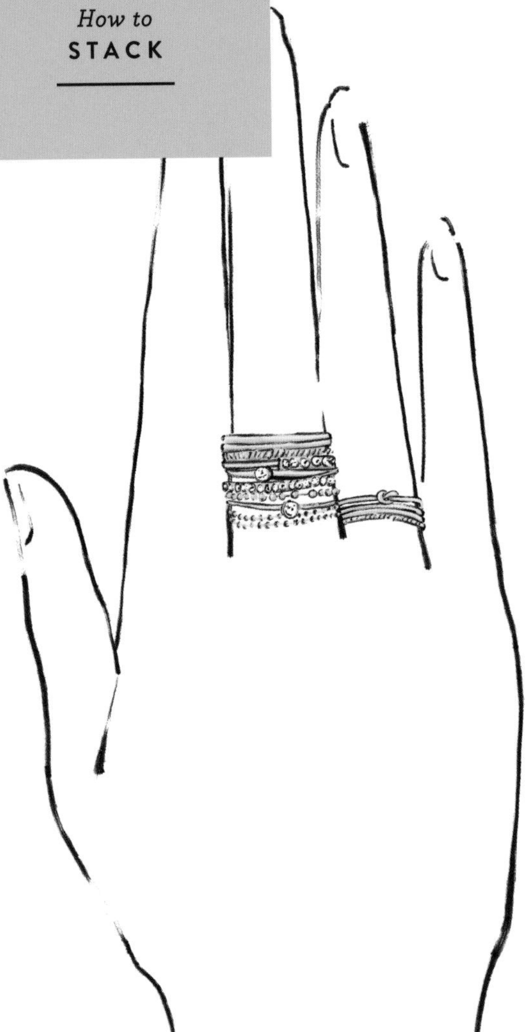

Even though rings are relatively small, they can have a big impact on any look. Make them loud and proud with an assortment of costume pieces or lean toward subtle and sweet with an arrangement of thin gold bands. Here's how to stack them up.

THE DELICATE STACK

1

Select your stackables. The key to any great delicate ring stack is texture and variety. Small chain rings, beaded wire rings, square wire rings, round wire rings, and small gem rings can all work in harmony to create the perfect power stack.

2

Mix them up. Once you have your collection of rings, it's time to get building. While there's no hard rule about the order of rings, it's best to space out different styles. For example, note how the gem and beaded rings are interspersed between the simpler bands.

3

Stack between the knuckles. The height of the ring stack depends on how short or long your fingers are. If you're going for a power stack (as seen on the middle finger), stay within the knuckles so that your fingers can actually move around. If you've got shorter fingers, this means your stack may consist of fewer rings.

4

Play with proportion on other fingers. If you have one power stack, keep the other fingers more low-key with two or three rings per finger.

MATERIALLY MAXED OUT

1

Select an assortment of statement rings. This includes costume pieces, precious gems, mixed metals, and interesting bands of varying widths. Commit to this curated hodgepodge look and go bold.

2

Pick one ring to be the showpiece on each hand. It's ideal to wear the largest statement ring on the middle finger so that the other rings can be styled around it. The showpiece on the right hand is the massive vintage three-stone ring. (On the left, it's the double stone on the ring finger.) Keep the right proportions by dressing around these rings with smaller pieces.

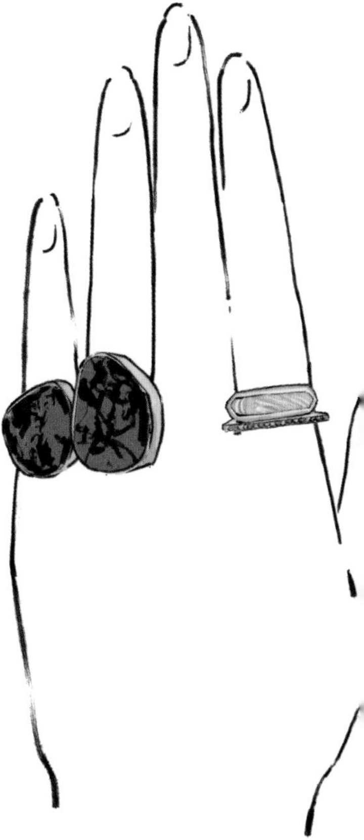

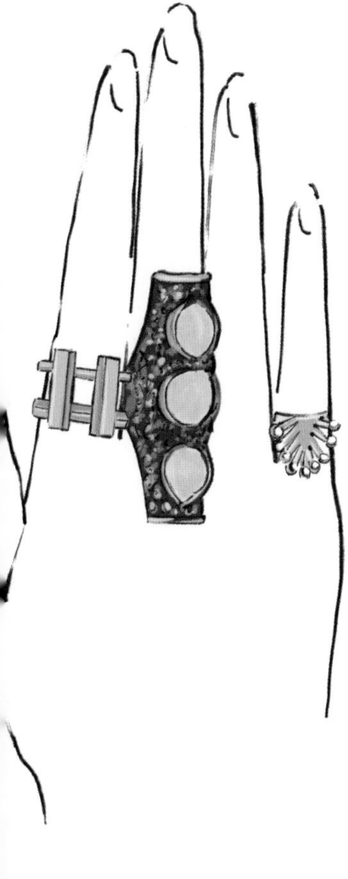

3

Double the fun. You don't have to utilize every finger (the unadorned fingers are just as important for balance), but use both hands for a maxed-out look.

ABOVE AND BELOW

1

Select your first-knuckle rings. First-knuckle rings, also known as midi rings, are the small rings that fit between the first and second knuckles of a finger. Most first-knuckle rings are dainty, perfect for wearing with other delicate rings.

2

Look for variety. While first-knuckle styles are normally thin, you can still find rings with various shapes to mix and match. Look for double-stacked rings, cutouts, and textured bands that have hammered or twisted metal.

3

Utilize all knuckles (not just the first knuckle). You can wear a first-knuckle ring solo, but it looks even better with a regular ring stack. Play around with alternating knuckles on different fingers.

4

Keep proportions in mind. As with any jewelry stack, be mindful of balance. If you're already stacking several rings on one finger, you will probably want to lighten things up on the next finger, stack a bit more on the next one, and so on. Just don't overload—keeping a few fingers naked makes this look that much more artful.

GEOMETRY OF RINGS

Consider these three easy geometric solutions to take the guessing game out of keeping rings proportional.

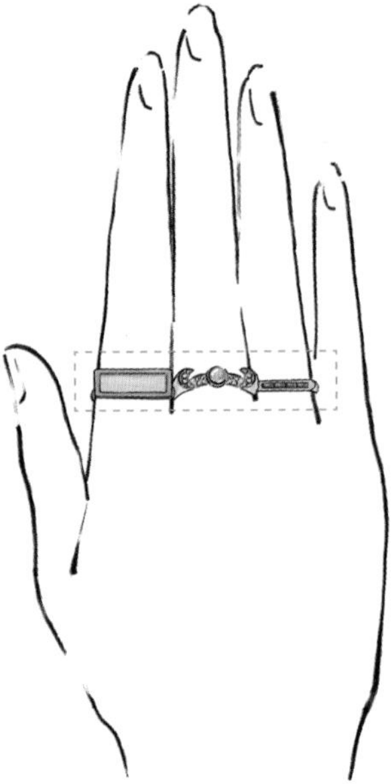

IN A STRAIGHT LINE

Wear three rings of the same width in a straight line—across your index, middle, and ring fingers. It's easy ring styling at its best.

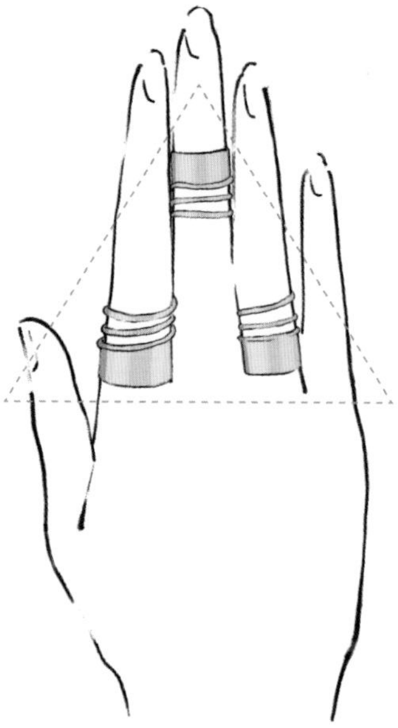

IN A PERFECT TRIANGLE

Select two rings, one for your index finger and one for your ring finger. Complete the trifecta with a midi ring around the first knuckle of your middle finger, and voilà—a perfect triangle.

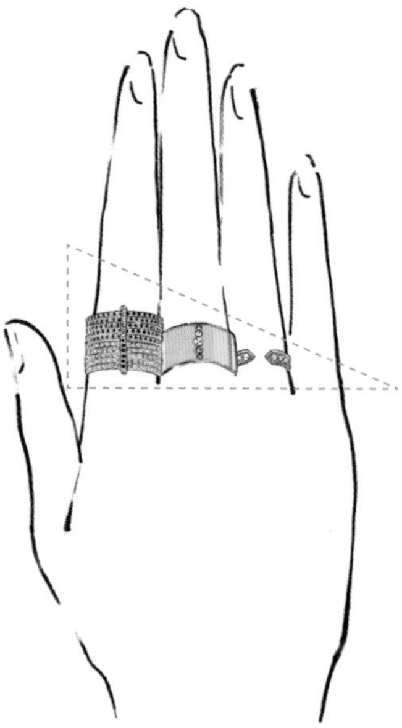

IN A RIGHT TRIANGLE

Create a right triangle by wearing your thinnest ring on your ring finger, followed by a slightly wider ring on your middle finger, and finishing it off with your widest ring on your index finger.

STACK
by Style

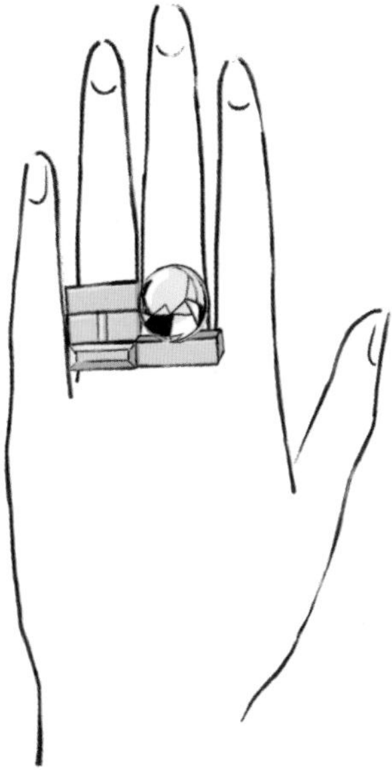

ARTFULLY MINDED ▸

Pair angular rings with a spherical precious stone to round things out.

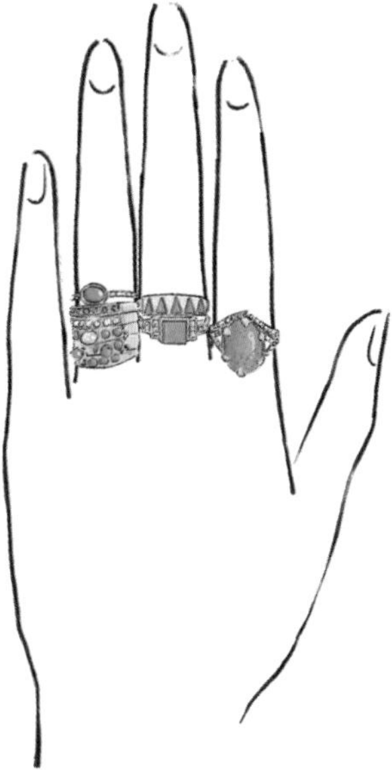

◂ CURATED GEMSTONE

Thin bands, Art Deco pieces, cocktail rings—as long as the gemstones are consistent, these rings will complement one another.

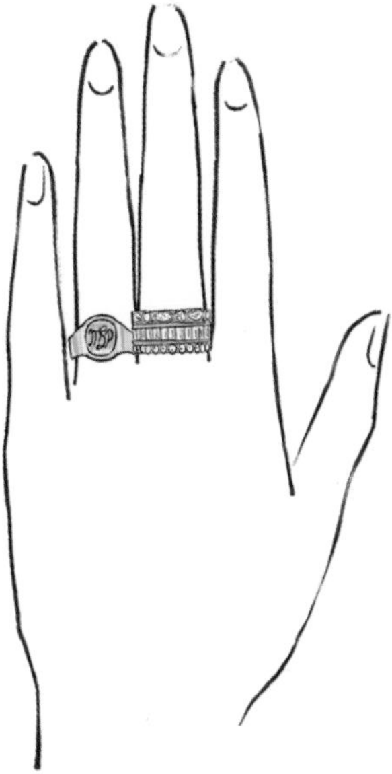

SIMPLY CLASSIC ▶

Nothing says classic like a stack of diamonds with a signet ring for a touch of personalization.

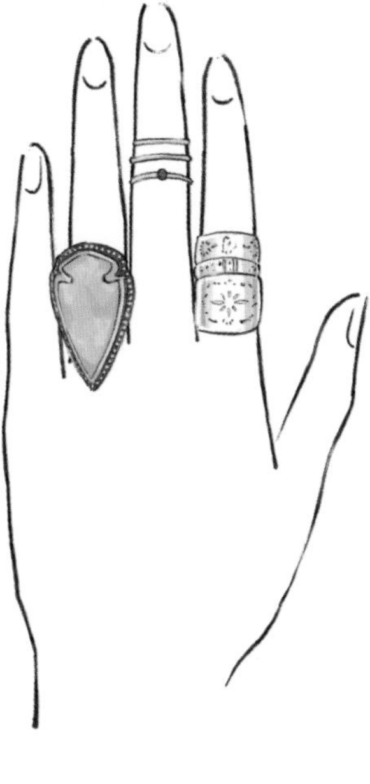

◀ **MODERN BOHEMIAN**

Go for bold ring cuffs with Southwestern-inspired designs to bring the whole bohemian vibe together.

How to Spot COMMON CUTS

	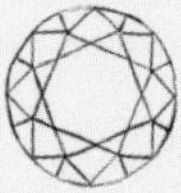	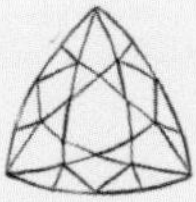
Marquise	*Round*	*Trilliant*
This almond-shaped diamond cut has the largest surface area for facets.	*The round diamond cut is the most popular and classic style—it was the first standardized cut due to its brilliancy and reflection of light.*	*This diamond cut refers to all triangular-shaped diamonds and can either have straight or curved edges.*
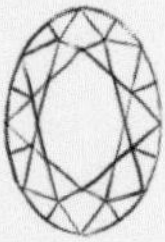	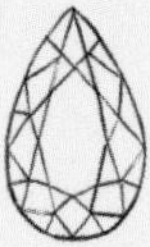	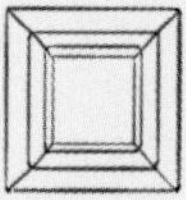
Oval	*Pear*	*Square*
The oval diamond cut creates the illusion of a large surface area and can elongate the finger.	*A hybrid of the round and marquise diamond, the pear cut usually displays excellent craftsmanship due to its symmetry.*	*A square-shaped diamond with step cuts means that the facets are more broad and flat, making the stone less brilliant than a stone with more facets.*

Identify the common cuts of your favorite gemstones with this handy cheat sheet.

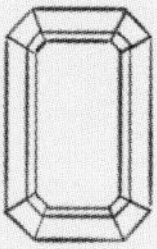	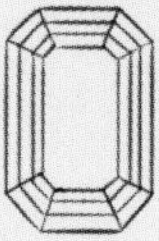	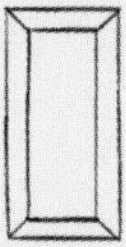
Octagon	*Emerald Cut*	*Baguette*
The oblong octagon diamond shape is similar to the square diamond when it comes to brilliance, but possesses more surface area.	*This classic step-cut diamond shape featuring a large, flat, tablelike face was first used on emerald stones.*	*This slender and rectangular diamond is the most common of the step-cut diamonds and is used as an accent diamond.*
	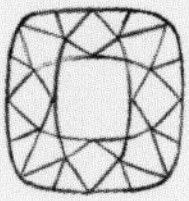	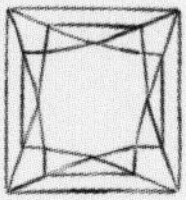
Tapered Baguette	*Cushion*	*Princess Cut*
The tapered baguette is similar to the traditional baguette, but tapers at the end.	*The cushion cut features rounded edges on a square or rectangular shape, giving it that antique feel of old mine-cut diamonds.*	*This second-most-popular diamond cut features the clean shape of the square cut, but has the brilliance of the round diamond with its many facets.*

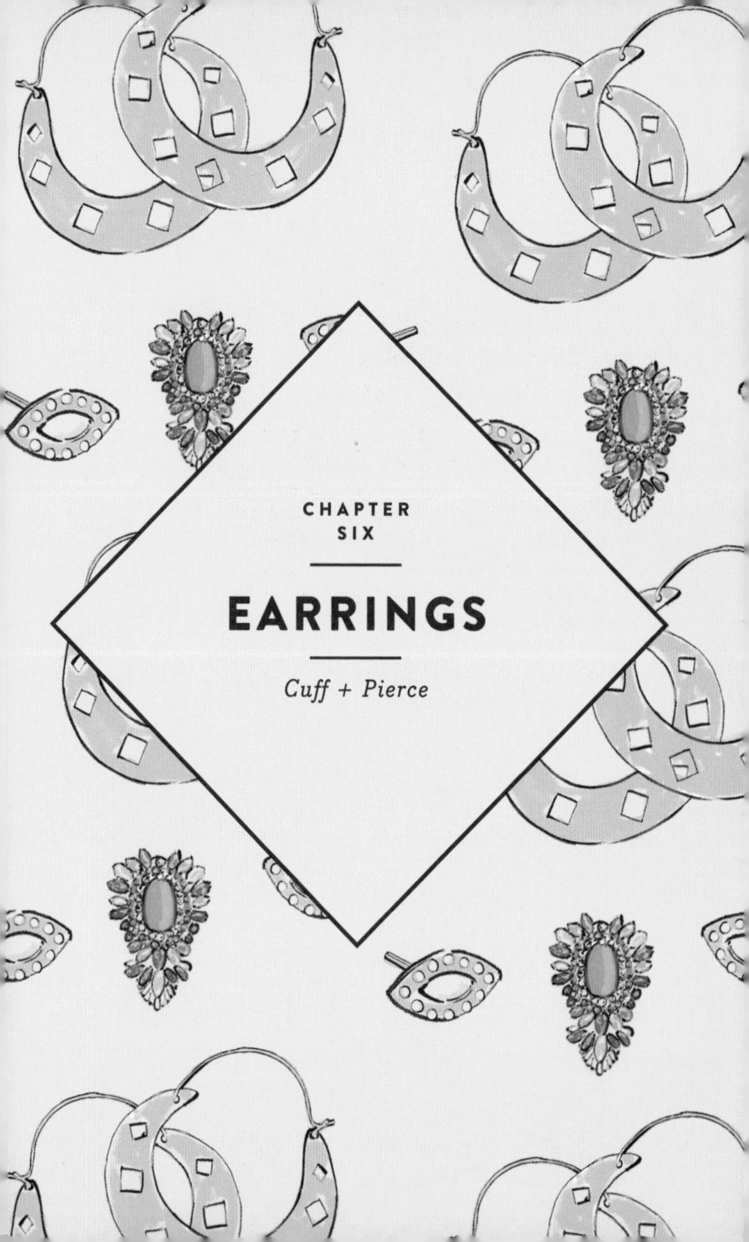

CHAPTER
SIX

EARRINGS

Cuff + Pierce

Earrings are totems of tradition, recorded as early as 500 B.C. in ancient Persian reliefs. Originally worn to symbolize status and age, earrings have evolved over time and across cultures to include a variety of distinctively modern styles, from ear jackets to drop chains.

Here are the most common earring styles to know:

STUDS—buttonlike, nonmoving baubles that stay on the lobe of the ear

DROP—earrings that hang from the lobe for a dangling effect and most commonly have fishhook posts

CRAWLERS—long and slightly curved earrings that climb up the earlobe toward the cartilage

HOOPS—circular earrings that connect through the lobe

CHANDELIERS—multi-tiered drop earrings that generally billow out as they hang and are often thought of as statement pieces

CARTILAGE—small earrings made specifically for cartilage piercings

FRONT-BACK—stud earrings that are decorative from both the front and back of the lobe

JACKET—earrings composed of a stud in the front and an ornamental piece that clips to the back and hugs the curve of the lobe

CUFF—wide, cufflike earrings worn higher on the ear to hug the cartilage

In this chapter, see hairstyle inspiration to match your earrings, learn to mix and match studs for multiple piercings, follow our foolproof method for rocking massive ear cuffs in a nonabrasive way, and more.

How to Style
YOUR HAIR *with* EARRINGS

THE STATEMENT CHANDELIER ▸

Statement chandeliers demand attention, so opt for a simple updo, like a ballerina bun, to make these jewels the focal point.

◂ THE BIG GOLD HOOP

Big gold hoops require zero fuss, so pair them with a relaxed ponytail for an effortless look.

THE MULTIPLE PIERCE ▶

Multiple piercings are all about subtlety, so why not go for a more complex hairdo like a side-swept French braid?

◀ THE MOONSTONE STUD

Moonstone studs may be understated in size, but their cosmic hues hold powers of their own. Make them shine with a simple pixie.

The New EARRING ESSENTIALS

THE CRAWLER ▶

The half-cuff/half-stud crawler earring is an elegant way to bring attention to your ears. To keep things interesting, wear just a single stud on the other ear.

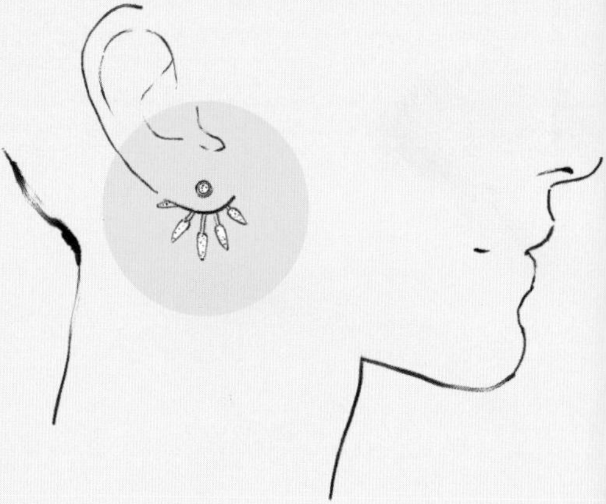

THE JACKET ▲

This two-for-one earring is a stud in the front with a jacket as an earring back. Keep it fresh by wearing it solo, or wear matching jacket earrings on both ears to edge up a more formal outfit.